Dedicated to the future of our planet, Earth; to
the readers of this book, and to the many wafers
of the realms of creativity....

ACKNOWLEDGEMENT

I acknowledge every muse that ever there was!

PREFACE

I have, for some time, intended to write a series of poems to illustrate my works of amateur art and plan a multi-media display of the works.

For most of my previous books of fiction, non-fiction and poetry, one has opted for the self-publishing route at the outset, primarily for editorial and post-publication control over the products, and also to expand one's outreach to niche areas of promise in the publishing world.

BookLeaf publishers appeared on my social media horizons, and I was drawn by the novelty of the idea of a 21-day poetry-writing challenge!

While these have historically not been the typical promptings for one to style one's writings into verse, the fact that I already had plans to write something tailor-made to go with my amateur artworks, blended with the intention to experiment with writing or showcasing a selection of forms of poetry, served to make for objective matrixes for an otherwise subjective exercise.

The poems use paintings that I've made over the years to pontificate over chosen themes and to add to the tapestries of one's experienced and written matter.

The themes of the paintings (and therefore the poems) revolve around Nature; Spirituality; Indigenous Thought; Law; Politics; Science; Literature and Personal and Extended History.

I literally penned these 21 poems in twenty-one days, though poems written and not published in the past would also have been accepted by the publishers. The last six or seven poems were penned on the last day of the #TheWriteAngle challenge, and hitting the submit button at the eleventh hour truly felt like an achievement!

This has been an interesting way to write poetry. As I participated in the July 2024 writeathon online from Gurugram, my mother's mother was on her deathbed in Visakhapatnam, Andhra Pradesh, and I heard of her passing away during the period of the writing of the book. This might help the reader decipher some of the tone and tenor of the work and its metaphysical conceits.

—   **V. Shruti Devi**

Index

Tarry, Tarry Nights

The highway's on a parchment
On a perch meant
for the negotiator
of paths

A road, a route, sparking sights
–Some of the darkest nights.

Cavernous chambers of the mind
–the inner eye
Project visions:
Light thrown
on ways
that catch the racing rays

Promises and visions
Saturate
Cascade, unroll….
–Signals to our times

Hurtling to the swirling nimbus,
those standing trees….
-Destination: Speech

Our minds are known
–the gauntlet's thrown
The electors, the elected
all sing one tune

–No barriers to breach.

By V. Shruti Devi

In the Galaxy

Kuru
Ca va
Say where

Wish I were
Say when
–the shores of time

Galactic
'neath Orion
Scrambling myths 'n' nebulae,
stars
Que sera sera

Betelgeuse, Isis, Noah's ark
A housefull tub
A grounded sub

We all are
the nuclear power

Tinsel, standstill
Stardust churns
'neath oceans, skylines,
pink sunset burns

At being museumised,
they'd all have turns
beneath Orion.

The periscope's upward crane
  plumbs the universe
    from its earthly plane

The seeds of all creation
    find their berths
Humankind oughtn't leave their hearths

Align these skies
in your planet's den
Enter a restful slumber
even before you can count to ten.

By V. Shruti Devi

Buddha in the Sky

5

The pages flutter:
Books on Zen,
Tich Nhat Hanh
Which chakra, which dhaam
or vihara
and then
some

Many-hued flags
twirl around those poles
horizontal lines
and yogic goals

Contortions of space and time
Herbs in the garden
Spencer's the line

Peaceful, eventful, giant outreaches
Moon-ward, star-clad
–sparkling wine

Glittering windows,
flitting jet
The heavens are busy
The makers are met

Within, without,
Reality emerges
–merges with Kirlian waves and dirges
sung to the moment, to the here and now

To reincarnate
as a new chant,
a ripple in space,
a plant

Moonbeam, crescent, primary colours, ocean's
                                    dew
Dark be the night,
–the luna blu

Molecular calisthenics,
Stellarine aesthetics
Wiggle-room
on the moon-bound broom
–sketchy

Ideas, magnetic meanderings
Skylines loom

The fragrance of the moon garden
Citric, white, to bloom at night
Skyscrapers smudge the solar view

Nebulae, supernovas, star systems, swirls
Sheer billows amidst elevated worlds

Spaceship, Earthship,
the voyages dawn
Earth to Moon
and back
upon the revolution

Starship, round-trip
astral planes
Travel made light with human brains
Humans to stay, humans to go
A touch of mechanical
a whiff of robot

Intonations inked on those rainbow flags
Sound waves, mind waves, electric rags

The more they fade, the farther they go
(the intentions made, the force of thought-flow)

Magnified by the moment, by the pigment
–Figments
The flower, the great chakra
churns the helminths of the brain
–squiggling
–Fruitful
O, bounteous moon
whence didst thou thine treasures fetch?

The ropeways to the Earth
Trapeziums of dotted shades
Slide to hills, to sapphire-lit glades

From craters to concrete:
Live monuments, sheltering fleets
of the specie
tech geeks, cyber gurus, social media rishis
that conjure, that meet
the drums of horizons
ever-expanding

By V. Shruti Devi

MARINE DRIVE, VIZAG:
Dolphin's Nose

A light-house appears
–pierces through the Dolphin's Nose,
the hill that's withstood
years of surf and sand,
docked seaward among its
spaced-out
peers
–Gently curves into the ocean
–Who set these lines in motion?

On the earth, on this artsy surface
Light skips light,
the creator's heart, a beat
Did intruders dare render this work incomplete
and puncture in this nose pin,
A Calcutta candy stick

–the Bay of Bengal,
Swirling gin
by Vizag by the bay.

The repeated light
Marked a place, a time,
  a regular evening sight

It came to be
—to wave ships off the jagged lee

Does it prevail
When storm winds wail?
Do fish swim up with prayer and plea,
Radiant?

Who drew the dolphins on a receding tide?
The nose-line fades into the old city
The burgeoning beach-line
—the behemoth
develops its way to a new aerocity.

By V. Shruti Devi

MARINE DRIVE, VIZAG:
Coconut Groves

As the Dolphin's Nose and dockyard
diminish in the rearview mirror
A look-east policy
by and large
(Ingressions, outcrops – Feng Shui would know
the stops)
would be in order to the right.

To the left,
Statues and a litany
of beach-road draws

A sea-ward crane
calls to sight
transplanted groves

Trussed-up coconut palms
Await their new-found fate
–to unfurl and to flourish
(which they did).

More appeared in droves:
Symmetrical coco plazas
–square feet now dot the shore.

By V. Shruti Devi

MARINE DRIVE, VIZAG:
Lawson's Bay

Past the city's elite
Ramakrishna Beach
the wheels roll on

The juggernaut of development
slaps a tsunami of a road
across our ear-marked lands.
Compensation?
Do clear that coast, O holy ghost! With solatium.

What a ship down,
a petition
up
whose street?

There's salt in the air,
a steady breeze
past Gyan Vilas,
the ancestral monument
frieze to frieze
Time was
An ancestor meditated
Undisturbed
and Attained

–was it
Samadhi?

One registers
one's mortal plot
As ships diminish at sea
and fishing fleets
present themselves
picturesquely

A hilly climb
by Lawson's Bay
(a pirate, legend has it)
Winding past
        dunes and stretches of ocean view,
Pathlets once led to streaky sand

We'd alight with picnic gear
Mats and beach buckets,
Sandwiches and tea-things
Not a human soul in sight
but the family band
casting footprints on the shore

The wave-break line,
jumping waves
gathering diverse shells galore

Jagged rocks
miniature sub-terrains:
warm pools
amidst crags
Insets of corals
spied at sunset
–the tongue of the sea,
cowrie shells, naabhi sea buttons,
conch-like pokey shells,
and what have we

Not a hint
        of human civilization
Not even from the
    fishing village
that assails the nostrils
en route
–where gliding through the
                    atmosphere
is a dried fish inhalation
that's bound to sublimate
into
the body's mantra-filled veneer
Oxidised, Iodised,
I inhabit these zones
And beyond.

By V. Shruti Devi

MARINE DRIVE, VIZAG:
Cyan Meditations

Across the hills and over the waves
The hypnotic buoyancy
of awareness
dwells
on impressions
–the hourglass a phantom:
–no co-ordinates, no dial, no moon-face
But granular views
of suspended animation

–The high gloss
of the ventral
side of a giant wave
as a surfer negotiates
an Old Spice ad.
How was the scene envisaged,
–When?
(I recall playing on the
    water's line
And being taken unaware
by a gigantic wave
–a towering wall.
With family around,
one didn't slip, didn't fall,

But it was a watershed moment
–the sea wasn't a breeze
the ocean's floor was steep
was the crux of that summer vacation)

–One had lived a tale
and would tell it.

Decades later,
A road slashed through
the precarious cliff-side
                              hairpin bend
The crag morphed
  into a park
and wings of steps
  descended
sea-ward

Predictably,
crowds began to manifest

At the base of that hill
One eventually did alight
I think it was 2010,
  in the early-morning light
  to do the Suryanamaskaar
And to chant the Gayatri Mantra
Unhindered even by the
          crystal japa mala

–Fortunately for me,
I had a family friend to count the beads
–a philosophical volunteer,
                    an aunt,
And another one
with whom I'd conversed
            the previous day
threw further light on my
                theories of breath
and chants
–articulating
"Yah Allah"
was also
a breathing exercise

At that post-dawn hour
As one did
God-knows how many
Suryanamaskaars
and rendered the mantra
into the dome of the horizon
In very considered, practiced, unique ways,
the hymn,
in my book,
acquired new syllables:
"Yah Allah!"

–I look heavenwards
and the "rosy-tinted dawn"

displays
the scribbles
of a jet-plane
flying north-by-north-west,
I suppose.

Clad in a flaming orange and yellow
two-piece swimsuit
from Greater Kailash, Delhi,
Energized, one began the ascent
                    back to the road
Engulfed in a blue tie-dye
wrap-around
The environ
caught the surround-sound

In retrospect
I believe
Baywatchers, cops, whoever they were
Did keep a wary eye
Even if from atop the cliff.

Cell-phone cameras
had not yet come into their own
But the sparks on the shoreline
might well have been in the line of view
of the International Space Station's crew!

This marked my thirty-eighth
trip around the sun.

A close-up of the planet's
aqua-lung.

By V. Shruti Devi

MARINE DRIVE, VIZAG:
The Bheemli Stretch

Before the advent
   of intricate signboards
   and signages
The hour-long jaunt
from Vizag to the town of Bheemli
was thought of
as Bheemli beach,
and pronounced
Bimli

Pulling beams
of light-house waves
    of rippling illumination
There once stood in B-town
a beach house, a palace of the
              nation
that once was.
–My mother's mother, the heiress.

For years, one passed by the ruins
while driving into Vizag
  from Kurupam
if we took the Bimli route

A scene
from a tragic Hindi movie
had been shot there:
Ek Duje Ke Liye (For Each Other)

This thoroughfare meets a dead end
                    in this town
—A recent discovery
while traversing these paths
to survey lands.
It re-emerges
in the avataar
of the East Coast highway.

But on the Vizag-Bheemli stretch
Deciduous ghaats
overlook the tar,
the sea-ward terrain,
the narrow sandy bar
before the high-tide line
the low-tide line
…there are Coastal Regulation Zones
that are in play.

On flatter stretches
you're treated
to navy-blue glimpses of the bay
the Eastern Naval Command holds sway.

Casurinas were once riddled
Into clearings after roadside clearings
You'd sometimes spot a stray vehicle
Around the Winter Solstice,
heaving home a maritime catch
—not a shoal of fish
but a trunk, a branch
of tropical greens
—Mistletoes to be adorned
with shimmering stars and cottony themes.

Where resorts and restaurants now capture the
                                    horizon
There once was a diversity,
a natural mix
of scrubby herbs and grasses….

The imagination puts acrylic to canvas
But would need to surpass
the artistic genius
of those who inspired this style
with palette knives and brushes:
Artists in the family:
—Glimpsing Greens by Kusum and Terraqueous
                                    by Preeti
Masterpieces and exhibitions
        of the twentieth century.

The impressionists were a major factor
A bard's eye-view,
–you get the picture.

By V. Shruti Devi

Antiquarian, Booketarian

Apt, then
that the image
that one focuses on today
is a view
of books
On this, the eve of Guru Purnima

A heritage library,
personal.

The ancestor who peopled
these antique shelves
with thinkers, healers, cartographers, poets,
                              playwrights
and their fancies' elves
Kick-started one's waking being
to the ways of Nature, humankind

Crumbling pages,
weevil-devoured
From dust to dust
proved in instant shards
of hard-bound litter

Sunning out the pages
–for not too long
lest the binding melts
lest the voltaic intensity
of monsoon storms
make short shrift
of encyclopaediae,
gazettes,
and solemn law books all in a row
–Even the world's first Oriya dictionary
penned by a relative of long ago.

Back into shelves,
solar-showered
Suryanarayana's trove
and more

Armies of 'modern' medicine,
Of modern political thought
Treatises on astrology, history, wildlife, art

Religion was a later shoo-in

One cut one's teeth
on Shakespearean delights
with Henry Irving's complete works
and an exhaustive microcosm of miniatures
treasured, gem-like.

The glow-worms
of brilliant minds.

He must've liked Tennyson
there's the complete works
and there's the complete works
—that explains one's partiality to alliteration
in the days of Wright and elocution,
a win-win situation
at least.
Though one was leafing through Emily's works
rescued from the stocks
of Sunday Daryaganj roadside strews
Looking for non-pedestrian verse
to toss into one's stew
with eye of sophomore, admission of
                              Shrew:
and waltz into hallowed portals
to be interviewed to read some more at SSC
from nineteen ninety to ninety three
—Three glorious years studying drama, poetry,
                              prose
Graduated with honours from Saint Stephen's,
                              Delhi
Gorged on samosas, burgers, gulab jamuns, and
                              neembu paani
—Fuel to interpret those fort-bound tomes
and tea

A book or few
made it to New Delhi
Talisman-like,
treasured
in book-cases from Lutyens' to Gurgaon and
Lutyens' and back:
from a series of literary works; the ubiquitous
                              Tennyson;
the Manufacture of Syrups and such-like

In years past
we've striven to preserve
the library,
keep the books in condition
–Shaking off pests,
lining shelves
through our south-bound homeward-bound
          summer, winter, and other vacations
–enlisting guests
if they were close enough and eager
to be a part of the ongoing mission
to save those volumes.

Some were brittle, some had stamps,
signatures and labels too
With bated breath, one scours type-sets for
                    handwritten notings (rare)
Over the years, we learnt a trick or two:
Dried tobacco leaves

are the best repellents
(of insects, rodents, reptiles, even)
Interested homo sapiens
do gravitate and peer
Sometimes startled by the snakeskin veneer
of those dehydrated arboreal placements
Smoking? You're joking!

Present-day publishers and authors
have been transiting into gaps
created
by the churn.

Our own writings (my father's book on electoral
reform; my solo works of fiction, non-fiction,
poetry and miscellany; my grandma's recipe
                                        book)
and books by people we know
–the intelligentsia
of twenty-first century India
and of distant shores

The Constituent Assembly Debates,
the Madras Law Journals
Cookbooks, magazines, mores and journals
–Shikaar tales, poetry, poultry

One's packs of tarot decks
and tarot guides

Books of mystery, of adventure: Children's
                                literature
And the comely Victorian romance or two

What you see in the picture
could well be a series,
a close-up
of volumes placed
on paper-lined shelves
Which have, on occasion,
made for
equally gripping reading
–a startling headline from a much-archived
                                newspaper
Those glossy old calendars
and rolls of brown paper
have found berths
on this track (stay away, weevils, we will be
                        back to rock you)

As the digital age
makes its advances
And one often sits at a laptop
surrounded by these depicted pages
–the library of my ancestor,
The Zamindar-Rajah of Kurupam,
One mulls over
commending selections
to electronic media….

Once-in-a-cyclone
whimsically crafting
one's magna opera
of recycled handmade lib. souvenirs

In some instances
Republication could regale the masses
—dispatched straight from the rural fort.

As we concern ourselves
with more haute
collections of reading matter
in the nation's present-day capital,
the Delhi NCR, Gurugram
At my sibling's,
Titles for children, young adults,
voracious readers. (And writers!)

Coffee-table books, biographies,
and, of course,
the cases of the Supreme Court
which, by now,
are all online,
and free
Though black-and-red volumes
line my urban walls
A bunch of cedar pencils
and cloves
keep silver-fish at bay

Zoom conferences, video calls
Visions surface in pools of lamp-light

In a zoom-in, you're transported
to the original spot
that evoked
the representation.

By V. Shruti Devi

INTERIM EPILOGUES TO OUR TEN-YEAR RULE:
Sea Haiku

Poll scenario:

A cross-current in the bay

—sea urchins' tarot

By V. Shruti Devi

INTERIM EPILOGUES TO OUR TEN-YEAR RULE:
Transit Haiku

Blueberry hills dash

–Go to Wolverton mountain,

violet's in vogue.

By V. Shruti Devi

INTERIM EPILOGUES TO OUR TEN-YEAR RULE:
Hairpin-bend Haiku

Forest vapours rise

People's voices have been heard

Workout: araku

By V. Shruti Devi

Chalice (A Sonnet)

An evening drive, a reservoir's a draw
Picture-perfect hillsides, hamlets tranquil
Sunset, flint-stones, boat-rides, houses of straw
Migratory geese, snail shells, photos to fill

Soundless waters, smoky abodes afar
Woodland ripples in the lake and the sky
Stillness, silence, clear air, quarries a scar
Almost pristine, weeds make bouquets –no why

Return to write, record the eve's pink glow
Sipping from an earthen tea mug,
                              pond-bath
In art, crystal lines are set to follow
trends of enchantment, rare golden star-paths

What's seen, what's heard, what's done by
                              human minds
Sometimes appears more fab in close rewinds

By V. Shruti Devi

Time Machine or L' Jawaab
(The Answer)

O mortal, mortal who didst write,
It's possible, you could be right
Some eternal brand and dye
Made grain and beast, diversified

Cocooned in their inner eyes
Sprang forth visions, fireflies
Dream-borne kings, queens on the wire
The Humane Band reached out higher

And science bolder, and unsurpassed
Conjured algorithms breeds apart
And though AI's heart sought to defeat
Homo sapiens knew their beat

Whose the grammar? Chart the plains
Which Authorities did one train?
A bluebird's feather, a goat that gasped
Crumbling castle, the interiors rasp

Drones rain down, reach out to peers
–"We're rich yellers with spears"
–"Wish we're not poor," I'm: "We're free
–Someone outwitted the laboratory"

By V. Shruti Devi

Formula Peace
(A limerick)

There was a fast bowler from 'stan

Rediscovered online, Oh, Man!

Epic speeches, polls

Siyasi, those roles

Now in stern pavilions; alleged scams

By V. Shruti Devi

Estate
(Written in Acrostic style
with alliterative inputs)

Larkspurs layered and swayed in the lull
Oriole, a golden oriole, and on a mag with the
          legend, Friend Request, an Owl
Delhi *deewaane*, O, in Lutyens' zone we did
                dwell
Irises, iconic florals, avians intel

Eagles, enigmas (invisible stars), the odd egret,
          euphorbias
Spinach, starfish, aquarium-creatures, sparrows,
          squirrels,
Tall trees, termites, clipped grass, hollyhocks,
          phlox, peacocks trending
Aloe vera, araucaria, asparagus, astounding aura,
          never-ending
Tip-toeing feline, bees in a beeline, tomatoes
          and tea-time
Endgame: Eureka! bird-baths, grains, –the
          mains: Earth Empire

By V. Shruti Devi

Aum Chanting
(In the style of a Pantoum)

I chanted, I painted, the Mantra divine
Began with *aum bhoo*, all that is
Micro, macro, elemental spine
Things as they are before they fizz

Began with *aum bhoo*, all that is
Then intoned *aum bhuvaha*, interactions of
matter
Things as they are before they fizz
Turn to blendings, mergers, imbroglios that
splatter

Then intonated *aum bhuvaha*, interactions of
matter
Before raising the level to *aum svaha*, the
interplay with one
Turn to blendings, mergers, imbroglios that
splatter
Mooladhara, Swadisthtana crossed, now the
Solar Plexus to stun

Before raising the level to *aum svaha*, the
                              interplay with one
Sounds purify nerves: electric, magnetic, there's
                              more
Mooladhara, Swadisthtana crossed, now the
                              Solar Plexus to stun
Stunned, rarefied, climb to *aum mahaha*, the
                              heart, the annahata's lore

Sounds purify nerves: electric, magnetic, there's
                              more
Aum janaha, the throat chakra, Vishuddha, blue
Stunned, rarefied, climb to *aum mahaha*, the
                              heart, the annahata's lore
Surmount it, and the voicebox will speak true

Aum janaha, the throat chakra, Vishuddha, blue
Paint splashes to canvas, synchronous creator
Surmount it, and the voice-box will speak true
Once it has, you're *aum tapaha*, ajna meditator

Paint splashes to canvas, synchronous creator
Aum satyam, truth, with starscapes, you may
                              now be in synch
Once it has, you're *aum tapaha*, ajna meditator
You've painted a graph, you're whatever you
                              think.

By V. Shruti Devi

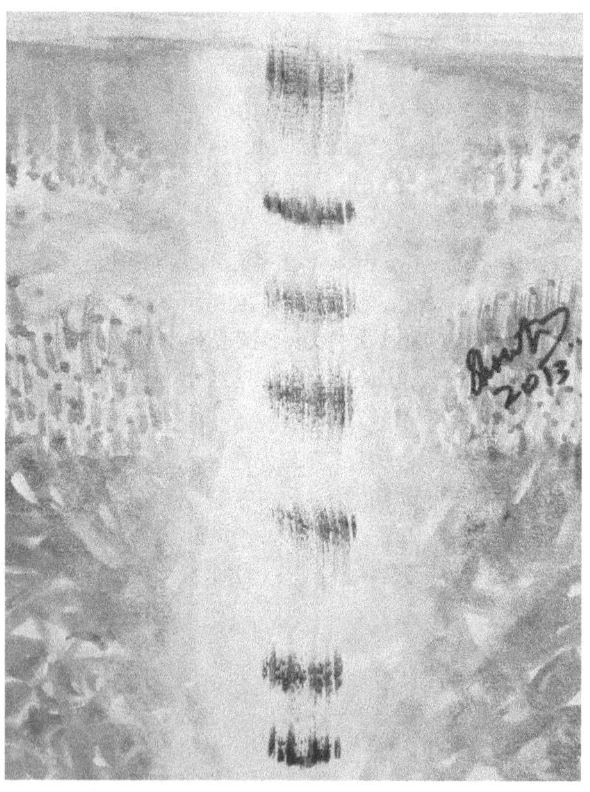

Stylized Waves: Climate Change Haiku

No climate fanatics here

—add it to the mix

Waves go chasing solutions….

By V. Shruti Devi

Ode to Technology
(In a diamante)

Tech
I hear thee
And we are enmeshed
Philosophers refined, and technologists
Geniuses, corporate czars, with propellants
Of various promptings
Temperance

By V. Shruti Devi

Ekphrastic, Do You See?

There twirl toddlers
  in party frocks
Balloons, festoons,
  pastel icing
Helixes swirl,
  Modern-day jukeboxes
Create waves,
  Occupy the air
Mosquitos hum
Blithe, light marshmallows
Mini dervishes,
atomic energy
Flouncy, cloud-like, intangible
Ekphrastics be fantastic
–Do we cater to accessibility?
Tactile, audible,
  braille-book tracks
–Read the confetti

By V. Shruti Devi

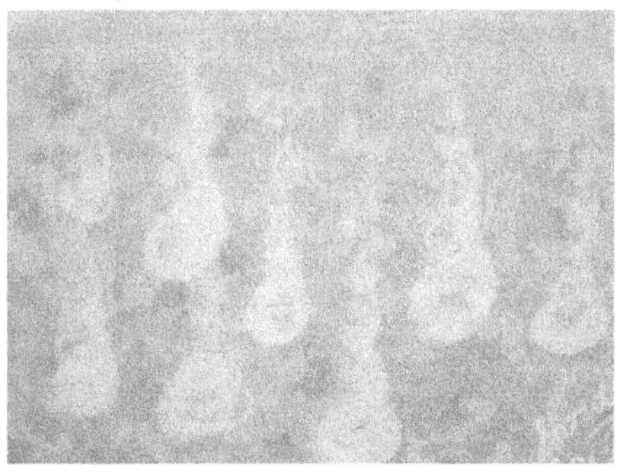

Happy Landings,
Developmental Blitz
(Based on the form of a Blitz)

Bombard development

Bombard education

Education with meaning

Education to free them

Free them, not make robots

Free them so they can soar

Soar to wherever they want to go

Soar to the moon, to space, or to no particular
place

Place the basics of healthcare

Place doctors, diagnostics, medicines, machines

Machines delivered by drones

Machines for telemedicine without depriving

Depriving them of their medicinal plants

Depriving anyone of ultra-modern remedies

Remedies of the law,

Remedies to access rights

Rights bestowed by the Constitution

Constitution of our Nation

Constitution as we interpret it

Interpret it and be sure to mete

Interpret it to mete out justice

Justice for you and me

Justice that will set them free

Free minds

Free people

People inhabit these vales

People expertly work these forests

Forests consist of diverse geographics, trees

Forests have definitions, have we made these?

These dictionaries

These pictionaries

Pictionary would do better

Better wall-art

Better craft

Crafting documents based on views

Crafting art-forms beyond paper

Paper tigers, real ones too

Paper planes to caper down

Down below, the woods approach

Down to the tarmac we do descend

Descend from the clouds

Descend from the fog

Fog out mosquitoes

Fog's not the answer

Answer the finer questions of culture

Culture's our dance

Culture's our gear

Gear up, it's the agency

Gear up for some uphill tasks:

Task One.

By V. Shruti Devi

www.ingramcontent.com/pod-product-compliance
Lightning Source LLC
LaVergne TN
LVHW021231200726
843509LV00012B/1472